Consciousness in the Sand

Fabrice B. Poussin

First Edition: 2023
Rs. 200/-

Cyberwit.net
HIG 45 Kaushambi Kunj, Kalindipuram
Allahabad - 211011 (U.P.) India
http://www.cyberwit.net
Tel: +(91) 9415091004
E-mail: info@cyberwit.net

Printed at Vcore.

Contents

1st grade soldiers

Little platoon of a reckless army
in uniforms of non-conformity
they march to the mess hall
it is noon again, training on hold.

Boys and girls in one battalion
recruited as babes in the crib
learning ABCs and one two threes
they wear dresses and shorts of khaki.

Fleeing the coop for a few minutes more
they rush to enjoy an hour of recess
the battle with books, pens, and maps
has ended with no one claiming victory.

Liberated they cackle cries of a ceasefire
there is no fear of an ambush for the moment
they share dreams, nightmares, and TV shows
shaping lives just beginning on the chalkboard.

Rain, sleet, or shine, they face their little days
disorderly children, privates in the first grade
with no concern for the next promotion
they strategize things no general knows.

100 More Years

The example is in infinite colors
sounds unheard in this decrepit neighborhood
scents made for divine creatures
it touches deep beneath the skin.

Bright lips of a never-ending gloss
though tight, speak in a thousand smiles
they bring comfort to the weary
in a solemn silence none can pierce.

Behind the glass the gaze is warm
deep blue after a thunderous night
a reassuring embrace surges
magical aura born from a noble soul.

Child yet he listens to her mysterious tongue
stilled by the strength of the daily teachings
if only he could live another century
grow with her words and apply her wisdom.

In the appearance of a puerile girl
far from the Amazon of ancient ages
all that surrounds her is awesome beauty
unassuming as she may be the giant in my breast.

6 AM

6:48 am… perhaps 6:52,
Little boy rushes to the kitchen,
hungry to be there for the big event,
like the first rays of the sun.

Focused on the morning sausage,
but ah! Morning no longer,
it started already 2 hours prior;
country bread in large slices.

Almost silence safe for the swallows,
in search of their meal also,
the cackling chicken and the rooster,
signaling a new day of Summer.

And in the kitchen, a knife cuts
through the sausage and bread,
focused on a day so long;
a day of noble tasks ahead.

Little boy sits too, smiles, silent,
eager for the life that always comes,
from the strong legs, the high forehead,
the rugged traits on a face yet young.

Fuel of bread, sausage, jellies and
not to forget coffee, black, mysterious,
certain in its goal to work wonders,
aroma, color, heat, and swirl rising.

The camera not there to snap
the photo of eternal memories;
Little boy knows, Little boy feels,
one day too he will share the vision.

7:03, or perhaps 7:05, one last treat;
the empty cup and a drop of brandy,
made of his hand like all else,
fruit of his heart, complete with his love,

Tackling life, without a smile,
the room is empty again,
his back, confident, walks away,
and disappears in a burst of light.

Little boy smiles with his heart,
the feast ended, the painting like
Corot's, has faded but not from his soul;
Little boy wonders when he will return.

Eyes lowered on an empty plate of crumbs,
the patriarchal cup and knife remain;
a tear of joy runs down his cheek,
thinking of this giant soul always at work.

His castle of dirt, and rocks, and sweat,
strong as the ox pulling his cart,
head down, not another thought runs,
but that of care which seals it all.

A Few Stones and a Prayer

The dreams of man a very strange thing
anchored upon the rocks of a dying city
they pray to carefully carved stones of chalk.

There is a realm beyond their horizons
calm and it waits for their wisdom
so close it only wants a moment of care.

But they walk on their knees and beg
before their own ephemeral creations
they can only see what they made real.

A fire burns within their weary eyes
and they cry surprised by their own deeds
for they did tear down their own palace.

A final gift

Under its plastic suit, transparent so it remains seductive,
with parallel burgundy lines, it lays inanimate,
enjoying creases straight, perpendicular, and oblique.

Unborn, though gifted with its limbs and bones,
it will not get a chance to stretch, evolve, grow old,
with its flat entrails, it lays as if hoping for a tan.

It will never know the hazards of a fast food meal,
nor the sickness of a few drinks too many,
gather the ashes fallen of an old Cuban.

To remain a virgin is its destiny, life of memories
never to have, no change, small or huge, to occur
in the last gift he received from the loving other.

A Million and a Half Guests

It the depth of the alcove
they came in great numbers visiting
in the thickness of the night
they rapped against his door.

There was a note in the morning papers
somewhere beneath the substance
of another close-out sale
in ink invisible as he had ever been.

Mondays had followed Sundays
regular as always unstoppable
and no one had remarked a change
next door in another secret alleyway.

It was said that it just happened
natural as clockwork on the implacable wheel
the fates had fulfilled their obligation
everything else fell into place.

A million little souls arrived at their appointed hour
to feed on the memories of this forgotten self
floating in perfumes made for other lands
like so many waves in the purplish veins.

Into a grey cloud of infinite storms
they move to hide a manic frenzy
and leave behind them but a broken frame
too frail for the image of the man he once was.

No one knew that something was different
a million miles away a butterfly expired
but those who call themselves his kin
went on with their eternal oblivious laughter.

Ancient Scholars

Dust plays tricks on their weary gazes
Alone in the ivory towers of their genius
The world may run topsy-turvy around their homes
Unaffected they seem frozen in the cradle of oldest dreams.

Lost in the midst of a cloud of stale smoke
Pipes lay cold atop the pages of an antique
Volume holding secrets of universes far away
In strange arabesques and magic formulas.

They may still smoke from time to time
Holding the rare cigarettes allowed by an old friend
Their hair grey for a little while longer
Floats above the vivid thoughts of their youths

Drinks have dried in the hazy glass
Cubes of ice wait for a spiritual marriage
As the light of those electric candles dim
On a world few still share with these relics.

Perhaps a last cigar will brighten the final years
Spent in secret within the oaken walls
Of a fortress built with decades of joy
In a thousand-year-old castle made for giants.

Those beautiful minds buried beneath the silver, the white, and
the bold.
Seem meek to the masses who have merely begun
Still, they hold the wealth of all generations
As they quietly conceive miracles for endless futures.

Atom in the Cosmos

Her soul is round
she holds it in her hands

She lives in a sphere
made to the size of her light.

Her embrace is a ring
of platinum and shiny gems.

Her breath is a bubble
floating on deadly storms.

Her essence is a circle
around the lost shepherd in me.

Her lips tender form an O
as she knows she is the life.

Her birth was a gentle shock
she continues on an infinite line.

A World Apart

Only A few feet above the sea
a bridge through the strange lands
of those who never truly die.

A road flows on through small towns
ran down by too many sorrows
wooden shacks creek in enduring agony.

The radio attempts to utter one last tune
along with the humming of soft concrete
like a funeral march under the cypress trees.

Streets lined with dying dreams of white picket fences
eyes onto those forgotten souls droop in rotten frames
hanging by the rusty thread of crying hinges.

At dawn the mist whimpers in heavy loneliness
at noon an eerie smoke hovers from cabin to mansion
dusk only brings the rest they so sorely need.

We continue the eternal journey through this wasteland
quiet as the aftermath of great battles
abandoned even by those who still lived.

Acid Campfire

It might be Tuesday in the midst of June
a calendar droops from a rusty tack
confused in its crumbling sepia tones
they can't quite recall who placed it there
or when, yet they have a vague impression
of a silhouette similar to theirs, decades before.

Someone set fire to a desk in the living room
to make a feast reminiscent of their teens
when they escaped to the dark forest
and sat around the makeshift hearth as magicians
when their dreams were still puerile
they could laugh without retribution.

It may have been twenty years ago or perhaps one
they have not ventured to the streets in ages
subdued by an existence without imagination
they slouch in boneless bodies
glassy eyes into landscapes no one else can perceive
they might well become part of the wooden floor.

They are five, perhaps twenty without a will
to stand or change the channels on the antique screen
they did laundry once and left it to rot
it was weeks ago, should they ask the neighbors?
but swimming through inches of dirt
wallowing in remnants of forgotten orgies they lay.

Someday their abode will implode
for a mistake under the expected influence
all who have survived will finally find a brutal end
in the flames of oddly concocted hallucinations
for a life without debt in a pricey world
too weak to face the humility of decent days.

Alone in the Green Room

It is a cold room of strange greens and creams
where you lay upon a steel alcove
given to the wishes of another morrow.

The silence is complete behind these walls
as voices in sober tones whisper in unison
words unknown to the loving heart.

Tubes of blue clear as a crimson cream
you gently inhale the air they made for you
so perfectly still in a mysterious night.

Shrill sounds pierce the waves of sound
a sharp light crosses through dimensions
burn away the flesh mutated to darkness.

You dream gentle spirit of another dawn
when you will sing to the many
who look up and seek your shining beacon.

Rest in the embrace of infinite love
soon you will awaken beneath a renewed sun
so we may utter these faithful words with you again.

Alphabet Soup

Playing with letters, mixing them all up in a dish,
I wonder how much they tickle.

What will they become under the motion, mixing
of a point so sharp, a dart of deadly curare.

No fear yet, in the game afoot on the shallow sea,
a giant crowd colored in a rainbow they look above.

The plot thickens in a milky paste of an ecstatic swim;
of love, murder, mystery, death, and resurrection.

Lines, of a wall of stones, a fortress in time,
it will carry through gravity, your name.

Hardened to become the shine of an unbreakable mirror,
silence may come to them, now set in their story, eternal.

Reflecting glass, passage, lifeline to the hungry souls,
they seem to dance, immobile, within a song from beyond.

No more need to stir, all has been written on the plane,
wave from your world to mine, solid and moveable.

The letters will not sign goodbyes, for there remains
not a moment to waste, eternity has come at last.

Apology

I set a fire upon your chest in error
it ravages within into glacial eternity

You once glided through the gentle paths
soul of a childbearing the flesh of a giant
an aura without questions embalmed
the seconds turning into infinity

Ashes set on your tender breath
heavy with the weight of universes

A dagger of invisible intentions stabbed
the simple dreams you endlessly harvested
the gaping wound expired in crimson
so many roses murdered as you wept

I do long for the return of this vision
apparition to scar the waves of time.

You will bear the mark of the accident
etched within all particles of your essence
majestic of powers unknown to the common one
mistress of the fire, conqueror of a private world.

Apple of his heart

A tomato
Red, plump
Stuffed
Fed by his hand

Steaming hot on a tray
And a smile
As he walks
And we are eager

Strawberries
In the sun
Fresh, fat
Full of sweetness

For us to pick
And savor
And a smile
For he knows

The garden of colors
With peas, beans,
Peaches and plums
And flowers for the bees

Love all around
In the Earth
And the trees
And he sits

A hard day's work
Beyond the years
Rain comes
The sun sets

Time for bed
And jolly dreams
Eyes heavy
And sighs to sleep

Under the dome
Two pyramids
And a cherry tree
The world he knows
And made for us

As the City Smokes

Staring down the wet avenue the revelers stagger
Ageless humans with forgotten gazes
Eyeing the body art they already forgot they purchased.

Yellow and checkered antiques zoom by
Splashing what they can of freshness upon them
Causing commotions of cackles and cusses.

It would have been a night to remember,
Stories for the books if they might only recall
Who was first to fall in the pool fully clothed?

Another day is about to begin in Gotham
In the alleys, the bodies will be buried quickly
For it is but an elusive hour when all seems quiet.

Subway vents are afire as if crematoriums
Of memories to be engulfed in flames
They smoke in wait of the next night to come.

A metamorphosis has commenced for these humanoids
Now standing upright with a more secure gait
As they enter the deserted halls to take them home.

Drained of all but life, they will dream upon the vinyl seats
Cradled by the steel wheels of their magic carriage
To awaken again under the gentle light of a friendly star.

At the crack of life

Lightning in the middle of lovely dreams;
rude awakening to the child in the night;
so small he surely did not imagine this fate,
to be a man when still learning to be a boy.

The deep of morning, rise and shine, the death
is to come to the chicks for it is their destiny,
still running around their lives, occupied
with the business of growing in the free field.

young life thinks, rubs the eyes filled with stones;
a long stretch, and the memory of what can be,
as it is each time. Fun to be had after all
With the big boys, the men, the dads.

Pride in the act, playing a part, actor of
so many lives; not seven, almost grown;
a task noble, discounting of course the birds;
he knows of the celebration to follow.

A day will be done, within hours not born;
trucks loaded, for a place unnamable.
as in medieval tales of knights an
maidens, hungry hearts satisfied.

Heavy lids demanding a rest, but for the joy
of the clan comfortably communing, with
not a thought for the aspirations of the fowl,
soon to walk the gallows of their written fate.

Battlefield

He fell on the battlefield of eternity
slowly onto the red dirt of a beloved desert.

Gently spun by a Nordic breeze he had an instant
to ponder the memories carved upon the air.

Soon the burning realm would mean little to him
behind the million-year-old dunes.

Often he had contemplated the errant's destiny
at peace within the ramparts of solitude.

Now the decay of a monument yet unfinished
began in the whisper of gentle sands.

A last feeble attempt reached for the towers
of the fortress crumbling into the heavy tomb.

The breast continued its fragile race
invisible already to the brush and its inhabitants.

One day he knew perhaps an unsuspecting saunterer
will stumble upon the ruins of this mysterious island.

Sleep comes now under the tepid cover of a dying fire
resting he imagines the first drop of morning dew.

Tomorrow will awaken without him
no one will sense his absence safe perhaps a void in the wind.

Because you asked

I give you pieces of time shiny and bright
on a platter of pewter and gold
incrusted with precious stones too.

Millions of years ago they say a grand old monster
gave its bones to posterity so time
would fashion a treasure in his memory.

It is a wonder in eternity that the eons did not stop
to contemplate what the elements fashioned
without aim for man to make a fortune.

Look now upon the glorious dress of summer
ornate with the gifts I made for you
gone some day in such distant times.

Old Dog

She ambles in the burning fields
a lab with the heart of a lion
hundreds of years old in her spring days.

Still galloping in hope of another game
she waits for the cry of the man
left behind ages ago when he tired.

Little remains of the days of glee
when they played with infinite joys
unaware of the dangers of solitude.

Now the moment of truth upon them
they face the fate of their kin
microbes in an unknown macrocosm.

He lags behind at the mercy of a wooden cane
while she calls his name in odd syllables
friends perhaps, yet alone in this realm.

One Little Death at a Time

A giant walking on the crowded avenue
sheltered inside a long coat
he seems oblivious to the great din.

Thousands saunter the common path
so many ghosts assailed
under a relentless rain of icy spears.

Weary of another day he returns home
abandoned by the gaze he sought
the asphalt heavy beneath the soles.

He knows none of the angry faces
haunted every instant of
what remains of miserable hours.

Resting atop the frigid shroud
a dark zenith looks down
as the body trembles with a final murmur.

It is just another common death
for this strange nomad
redundancy of a day already lived.

Packing Lives

She walked in the middle of my life
with a suitcase full of hers;

I barely noticed
when she moved my things around.

and a drip in the bathroom,
drop in the kitchen,
flood into our days.

So she walked out in the middle of my night
with her suitcase and one of mine.

Papa's Old Place

Looking for Isadora on the boards of a grand opera
it is a store of shoes on shattering sales she found.

Hunting once more on the shelves with Hem's Nobel
what remained were windows to dusty piles of stationery.

Seeking a teacher with soft brushes and palette
to discover barrels of bland paint in Mary's stead.

No more gentle smokes in friendly clouds
above the souls of those vanished geniuses.

The monument Gertrude was on the old sofa
now a still marble upon a forgotten mantel.

George too a ghost behind the curtains of his symphony
a bad haircut in the wind of those great turbines.

A man with a camera master of rays in all lights
the poster in the doorway, no one can name yet.

Lives in a time forgotten birther of a present unknown
they haut every inch those today cannot deserve.

I search in every crack for a sign of those I love
they are buried under the rush of days without soul.

Cobblestones of blood, street corners guarded by none
avenue wide as uncertain crevasses into Hades.

The city is living in a state of permanent death, cold
as the memories survive in the misery of meaninglessness.

Walls of glass, stone, and concrete, sky of cold steel
the arteries are hollow, devoid of warmth and motion.

I remember those I never knew for their passions
they linger within my fibers, and the city seems to be.

An illusion it is; I lay here in my tomb and fancy
with those friends, when still there was life intra muros.

Polka Dot Suit

Leader of the team
rich as Croesus with gold bullion
and a silly red plastic nose
he reigns at the top of the empire
one thousand feet above his childhood
and he dreams.

Monuments could be built
to the ties of silk and platinum timepieces
as statues sit poised for another merger
spying a copious breakfast made for kids
he smiles in his wealthy souls alone
in a polka dot ensemble.

A shock to the system late again
scraggy hairs throw rays of light at an audience
somewhere hovering between youth and death
he had to dance all night in his living room
as he continued to sing an awkward tune in the bath
much too young yet to play with the board.

Leaning back in the presidential leather
teasing the graying beard which never really grew
he is again blinded by the shine of intimidating portfolios ·
wondering what migraine those executioners
have in mind for his playful little soul
he might cry, instead, he chooses to smile.

Trickster with castles in Europe, he stares at the water
in a carafe he wishes would explode and ruin
all those reports. He hopes his chair would break
so he would fall back in a loud commotion
but then he knows, only he would rejoice
so to sleep again he goes into the din of the boardroom.

Portrait in a Door

Clusters of words swirl in the depth of a strange realm
images flash to make motion of what was once so still
stories emerge in endless chapters of sobs, grins, and laughter;
conversations stack scatological through a fertile desert.

The apparition endures less than a moment
a single frame of utter simplicity to be held in a safe
a soft breeze penetrates with the slow motion of the gate;
waves pass gently through the ebony sea.

An aura comes to be borne and stills the hour
which needs no more to hold with a meaning for millennia
impressionist with the glow of Degas' juvenile dancers
rich with life for eternity in most intense serenity.

The hand on the frame which soon will close
gliding as if to the fragile envelope of the infant
her face remains in a tilt as she dares a light smile
she seems to speak, but sounds are trapped in the canvas.

Deep blue crystals to a profound soul gape to her will
the pose becomes imprinted on the unseen frame
a memory laden with the ongoing present
she creates the impossible, never to perish again.

Reading the silence

Never will I tell you
all my thoughts

Never will I make it clear
or obvious

Never will you know for sure
what I meant to say

Never will I use every word
for you to read

Always will I leave blanks
and unfinished thoughts

Always will I ask you
to come in

For my home,
my heart, my soul,
my thoughts too can be yours

But always you must reach out
to find, and read them

Those words I cannot think;
these thoughts I will not write

For never should you expect me
to know all, and say all

I am only a beginner of ideas,
a planter of notions

Always you must fill in the blanks
for I need you to speak,
also.

Remember

Remember the days of hopscotch
playing house with your mother's dolls
putting on a grandmother's old dresses
and at last, trying just a little foundation.

You smile at those past decades
little girls mirroring what you once were
they giggle with a tickle of a mysterious touch
perfect triptych of a thousand old years.

They have grown from the days of a twinkle
close to the flesh whence they emerged
warm and tingly of a beat still within their breast
little ladies soon to go through the metamorphosis.

Still the same in your intimate fibers
as in the moment you brought a little more joy
to a world a little less empty for the moment
you do recall the butterflies deep within.

Child again, little lady forever to come
grown-up for all those around to believe
you tiptoe about the years of the woman you might be
the universe of the ageless to be yours for all times.

Great Little Friend

Do you remember the tight embrace
in those days of sweet nectar
when the games of youth were all we knew?

Have you forgotten the caring glances?
as a fiery sun blinded our laughter
now so much later into the night?

Are you lost at dawn facing the bay window
gifted an apparition in the gentle mist
a fleeting memory of our days on swings?

Perhaps electricity still runs through
the virgin tips of those digits
strong to make you tremble with fearful joy?

I imagine you now as this earth closes in
in your dress as a spring garden
running to me your dearest purpose.

We were so light then you and I
carefree women not even teens
in an eternal giggle without cause.

I hope our final tears linger upon your cheek
the death of childhood the end of the affair
alone in the world loving as pure souls must.

Do you remember the tight embrace
our eyes closed onto our many mischiefs
as we watched the world go by a stranger?

We played this odd symphony on the grand
mimicking the waves of a distant ocean
I fancy it resonates forever in your breast.

I touch the single photograph of us
to find myself with you again in the meadow
my chest heaves in joy at your touch from above.

Feet dangling over the abyss to this earth
I imagine I will soon sit with you
in the dress you offered me with a wink.

Remembering Hopper

It is easy to remember the artist
of colorful diners lost in a low neon glow.

It takes little effort to recall the words
of the poet who sat alone in a forgotten eatery.

So many have come and gone through those doors
revolving from one lone moment to another.

Their shadows continue to haunt the leather
of worn-out chairs where a dying cat slumbers.

Signs have faded under the hailstorm
wooden steps rotten to the weary traveler.

But to the spirit of the one who never left
the scene is too familiar to vanish from his fibers.

It is his life carved in true sentences
his tears painted upon the veined canvas.

Too well does he know what it means to be lost
as he stares at the benches by the night.

Reunion

One reaches closer to a star, years ahead
two race to catch up in this vibrant day
three struggle for a breath, lagging a little.

Seconds dripped slowly a grain at a time,
in an hourglass in truth counting eons,
unable, perhaps unwilling to up its pace.

The road of winding curves and traitorous
peaks, came alive, to frustrate a joyful ride,
so long awaited, as millions passed by.

Warm nest of the two when days were younger
not one is ready for them to fly the coop
home is still theirs, walls nurturing them yet.

A force of planetary magnets comes to be,
for a trio to once again take a long stroll
two stand at attention, holding out their hearts.

Little souls need their heaven where all is cozy,
neat, and wraps around their tender flesh,
a blanket fit for only them, pulsating with her life.

One steps out, the journey to an end at last
two are all smiles, in every cell, every membrane,
a sweet song emerges in sparks as they run.

Three are one again, soon to return to the fortress,
where no harm will come, they embrace
a sigh reverberates, heard at the far end of the era.

Riding the bicycle

It is hard to ride a bicycle with a child on the back
the man cries obscenities for he knows no love
little boy sits, tight behind the giant, and smiles
what does he know of hate, jealousy, and the Reds?

Gray top, close to the ground, narrower of mind
screams words he cannot possibly understand.
What does he think he knows? Old man lost in nothingness
tonight he will beat his son silly again, for kicks.

Now, we pedal down the path to the river, under fire
you will die he says, firing squad will be your last meal,
I tell you so for I am ruler of all things in this land,
I own acres you realize, and a wife and a son I can kill!

Little man, five from his birth, wants to giggle on the seat
the giant ignores the monster with vile teeth
he is aware of his own power, strong, needing no one else
the world vomits as the dead man continues his rant.

How do you survive the killing bile of cyanide and sulfuric acid?
half little man will not forget the threats of a crazy old one,
who for fun has nothing but violence on those he loves
rest in peace now Mr. Neighbor, your time is done!

To the river, to fill the troth of the milky ones of black and white
far behind the yells of a cancerous heart, plagued to the bone
throw your darts, and fire your canons until the end of times
lucky perhaps, I will lend you a hand sometime.

Days are forgotten, years to a little guy now grown a bit more
a single faint memory of Mr. Grumpy who killed everyone,
in blue overalls, what was he thinking with his shoe in his hand
to the face and head of the boy name Roland or a legend?

Forgive ignorance, the old man has passed, so has the knight!
Charlemagne sobs on a scene of sorrow strange, corpses many,
and man-child giggles at last, for the giant tickles to soothe;
it can be hard to ride a bicycle with a child on the back.

Road to nowhere.

Sixteen streaks of life on a frozen highway
a last thought on a road through paradise
school was out at last for these eager hands

It was time to race with the men
to the wonder of a promising dusk
greasy fingers, feet by the hearth.

He dreamed of a mere existence under a shack
home for the simple mind filled with glee
a can of soup and the second half of a squandered cigarette

Someday he would enjoy the welcome of a friendly canine
sit back as colors above turned to black
and finish another Marlboro forgotten in a rusty toolbox.

He went on with the same carefree joy riding shotgun
in a pick-up kept together with an extra coat of paint
winter came to greet him with unknown gift of Christmas.

Laughing on his way to a broken furnace
his throat to the glass when all came to a stop
at the end of sixteen candles broken in mid-flight.

Ages have too died since and I go to the stone
a faded image of the lanky pal
I hear him giggling on the playground still.

Rolls Royces and little yachts

Dressed in a bright gown
feet in golden stilettos
she stirs the Lamborghini to a halt
near the Cartier store where she will splurge.

Not far behind her the smoke of a city
fallen to the greed of the would-be gods
a low cloud hovers thick as muck
heavy with the weight of infinite miseries

The tuxedo waiting for her, too dreams
of helicopters and private jets
lounging on the acres of his vast greens
one step closer to vast fortunes.

Descendant of royalty long forgotten
little, wrinkled by endless suns
alone in the dingy room, she cleans
mansions and castles large as her city.

In thousand-dollar Hawaiian suits
others bask on the beach of their own islands
fake hair and skin made of silicon they also go
to the tomb… in million-dollar outfits.

Rush Hour

I remember
how can I forget
I had just learned to walk
just opened my eyes
just learned to live.

I was happy
running around your days
it was simple it was sweet
I had it all!

So soon it seems I woke up
it was rush hour
all around
twelve lanes of mad racing things
I was all alone.

Over the days when I was
running around your life
you left me there
at rush hour.

Birds of Prey

Permanent as the depths of space
a dark cloud hovers over the crowds
fragile in their naïve innocence.

Animated with the dreams of a morrow
they take their place in the flow
of eternities marked upon their streets.

Thick as an ocean of tar the mass follows
from above at a safe distance glaring
like birds of prey for the weak child.

In turn, each will pounce and take a life
entrusted to them with the kindness of submission
cheated by a promise to protect and to hold.

Still wet with the first lights upon their skins
they have surrendered to these black vultures
mistaking their fiery glance for a noble oath.

Now the storm attacks as a vile battalion
without mercy, it will devour all that it touches
to leave behind but a field of horrified carcasses.

Black Out

Precious moment at midday when all stops,
home for fuel for beast and boy, a privilege
to play with the big ones, and feast with them.

August has been a scorcher and makes no apology
for the sunburn on an exposed nape, or the dust
on a sweaty shell covered in balm and salt.

Soup with ice and sweet sugar, and toasted bread,
a hearty slice married to creamy butter and sausage;
a roast full of tender juices, enchanting herbal aromas.

Dessert of fleshy strawberries in ice-cold, sweetened
juice of grapes, to crown the achievement of the lady;
grownups will have java in a hurry before they nap.

Eager, little boy climbs back on his steely steed,
in love with the thick air of a heavy afternoon,
cozy in a great desire to slumber in the heat.

The heart roars, the blades cut deep through the Earth,
while a dream of a humming chopper keeps him alert,
and the certainty of a great adventure on the tube tonight.

In the hay, under the starry barn, a best friend at his side,
the hero takes thirty, luxury he must afford, gift of the day,
eyes shut, so far away, what were his dreams?

Body Parts

Bewildered upon the speedy delivery
a gift from an untimely Santa Claus
the box appeared in silvery wrap.

Eager as the young explorer
of unknown lands in hidden realms
he cherished the moment of contemplation.

The box came alive before his little soul
to reveal the secrets of one hundred years
and twenty more under a darker light.

Neatly arranged in silky compartments
parts found themselves set in motion
seeking the safe destiny of a brethren.

Yet a sparkle of another's dream
he imagined a statuesque ideal
standing atop a peak of his own making.

It was he waiting to become
the sum of infinite experiments
aiming unaware to an end in perfection.

Body parts, complete and ready to assemble
things that would never really be his
borrowed so he too might play his part.

Cadillac Emperor

Yesterday a Cadillac, today a Land Rover
gadgets galore even under the leather seats.

The wheels roar passed the last curb of green
nothing can slow the emperor's coming.

Like a siren from Hades a horn clamor to the peak
as terrified peons make room for the crazed apparition.

Upon the black mat, he will step, smart device in hand
important as if royalty upon a Hermine path.

Scanning the surroundings from those six feet to the skies
even the fearless critters freeze in their steps.

There is no escape for those in their rusty Pintos
it's live or die under the ruthless fist of the ruler.

Refuged in the borrowed palace he surveys the realm where
none should move if he wants to remain in his dangerous clutch.

This king reveals orbs of fiery red in the frigid room
surrounded by so many cadavers fresh as the morning dew.

Alone at the command of the monstrous carriage his world
he frowns to maintain a steel hold on the meek souls.

Carnival 2020

Mardi-Gras in April
extending those days of glee
when revelers saunter the avenues
seeking another merry melody.

Yet they lack the luster of old
hiding in shame behind blue fabric
they wish they might breathe
inhale forgiveness in the shadows.

Stumbling in fear of the unseen
they stare at their kin on the other side
smiles erased by the feeble mesh
pleas fleeting within their breasts.

Pastels will quickly fade in the rain
sad reminders of brighter omens
ghosts soon to outnumber the crowds
amid clamors echoing into the void.

Chimera

Old man on a rocking chair, swinging,
sleeping.

Resting,
flashes of a past that never was, ahead.

A glimpse into a future without return,
wishing.

Thinking,
too late for the dreams never reached.

The girl of eight laughs in his ear, singing
Dancing.

Tossing
the baseball, the brother of ten warns.

At two scores and more, she is beauty,
caring.

Loving,
gazing to the old man of the rocking chair.

She smiles, sparks in her eyes reach him,
longing.

Dying,
a last vision of a reality only imagined.

Chrysalis

Tight within another skin
her essence smiles inside
warm in the safety of the forest
she awaits the moment to emerge.

Wings like hands in a prayer
she moves as if a wave in the walls
the body liquid with grey matter
eager to become bone and be free.

Through a gentle membrane, she lives
a new heart pulsating in those clouds
made of ancestors but a day old
in the light, she glows strong as a star.

Soon she will plunge into this life
simple in the invisible apparel
I will catch her before she falls
to save her from a hungry earth.

Coffee Shop Stories

These two hide little of their privacy
comfortably slouching at the coffee shop.

They have amazing stories to share
with each other for the world to know.

Little turkeys gobbling under their crimson hats
singing virtues of the newest office gossips.

Fat hens they cluck away family drama
in the high pitch of a spring fair vendor.

Hiding beneath the fancy dresses they continue
to declaim inanities made of unknown sounds.

But they will leave as they entered, filled with a million prides
their heads in the heavens as they continue what they think a
hymn.

Coincidence... again

Few climb those hills any longer, for you see
life is so comfortable in the valleys where
no surprises haunt the steps of the meek.

If only they could imagine the ephemeral moments
carefully manufactured by a mindful universe
there for the taking of those who merely venture above so
briefly.

Lucky is she who finds a little courage
an instant passed midday to hike the trails
and bask in a sun made of stories for the taking.

Invisible against the pure sky of ice
she continues on, firmly to her destination
a dream only she sees within her grasp.

Unexpected encounter made in her world
perhaps he too wrote a scene or two
for she slows her gait to gently stop and smile at a vision.

There is no coincidence, a voice uttered in the deep
no chance meeting when you reach the heavens
no more illusion when following the written path.

Consciousness in the sand

Pounds of gold in the sky
for gilded days to extend
to a certain eternity they can afford
on the souls of the billion poor corpses
they trampled along their march
for fame in dusty history books.

It is life they seek
against nature as even stars perish
since they believe it is the privilege
of the rich to prolong their years
them who did so much to advance
progress and leave behind those who made it possible.

With fiery gazes flowing in evil arrogance
they claim their entitlement to the universe
so they will make new bodies for themselves
save precious moments into the sand
without feelings or sensations, they will
lie awake for eternity on a bed of wires.

Perhaps they missed the dreams of Shelley
Stoker, Rice, and their worldly cohorts?
Have they not seen all the shows
haunted by human monstrosity and the living dead
when even ghosts of our ancestors tremble
and heaven's gate threatens to close.

We may go to a place where no man has gone before
conquer planets and even galaxies far away
but I fear we have been told by their erudite friends
men of deep science with bulging wallets
that even the sun will someday need eternal rest.

So goodbye I say to these men
who claim a right above all humankind
to establish misery throughout the realm
so they may swim in endless seas
with two or three of their wealthy brothers
and never again know the pleasure of suffering.

Contemplation

Leaning onto the high metal fence,
morning and evening, he watches his work,
wondering of the outcome.

Surrounded by a menagerie of hundreds,
friends, for a moment, accomplices
his desires, his passions, only to do good.

A field of wheat, wave under a kind breeze,
hoping for rays to turn it to gold,
bread of our days, dessert to many souls.

Corn all around, with hairy cobs, fairies of his land,
thirsty all the week-long, growing to eight feet,
forest of tickly giants, proud to scratch the azure.

Prisoners under the caring gaze, they move slowly,
sandy tongues give thanks with a thick wide lick,
their future certain, but bovines can't tell forth.

Leaning on a wooden fence, his thoughts at rest,
wheels turning as ever, he ponders the crops;
life will go on yet tomorrow, without a doubt.

Crack in the door

The blouse rests neatly in the sterile armoire
she neglected to button to the neckline
only a few hours ago when she returned
home from a journey never to be denied.

The hours have not yet gone to rest
a light continues to shine within the strands
the joyous silk still dances in its home
exploding particles lag behind alive yet.

Hand upon a breast the body sleeps
teasing the edge of the abandoned garment
in the complicity of old friends after a fete
darkness has set across the rooms.

This night she will dream of freedom
the skin caressed by the warm color of lights
beneath the tight-knit of a reflective armor
a thin fortress she desperately longs to shed.

Crosses

They display a temporary faith about their stuffy necks
while tattooed upon their flesh a reddish swastika
loudest in the children's park they throw away
empty cans of light brew they crush with their skulls.

Barely seventeen she passes a weary hand through
the black curls pampered by years of kindness
remembering those brown-eyed girls who burnt,
suddenly unable to smile she trembles.

Heavens darkened in her sunniest of afternoons
a frigid blast violated the privacy of her bones
staring at the feast a mother offered
she no longer found a need to partake in the joy.

The gross clamors of that neighboring clan
stabbed at her soul as if she were on the stake
but she saw the cross again around their necks
become a noose and gag their arrogant utterances.

There was hope, she thought.

Dark Armies

They have arrived
monsters under cover of three pieces
including tie and a good old book.

A great star of light and life still shines
far above the darkening land
perhaps it waits to pounce at last.

They are closing on to the innocent
faces of grins and mocking smiles
as they take another step too close.

Skins ooze with a stranger perfume
bellies swollen by decades of self-satisfaction
legs wobble under the ignorant mass.

Fist of fat fingers in the air almost unable to close
they protest and scream at the living
who still believe in loving a neighbor.

Speaking mighty words twisted into lies
of course, only they know the truth
that it is others who hide their ugly souls.

Under semi-human features scarred by their blindness
they point accusing cannons and semi-automatics
at those in sterilized outfits.

Since when must the good die
at the hands of such evil, attempting
to take over a world surrendered to unavoidable death.

Monsters on two varicose-infested legs
speaking the tongue of tyrants
their pleasure in the demise of the gentle multitude.

They are here with their vociferous blaspheme
speaking in the name of a god they ignore
until he too will perish in the realm.

Death in shock

The creature in the black robe stood holding her faithful
scythe.
Greeted with loud laughter, it appeared stilled,
the unusual response enough to quench its mercilessness.

Divine mathematics

Enamored with chalked-up equation
Relic of a century-old explanation
She stares into the void beyond the wall
To discover the proofs of the great philosopher.

Dream killers

A little prince in broken-down shoes,
he did not know what royalty might be,
living below the moats of the old citadel,
dwelling under a slab of mud and bark,
sleeping of the dreams of sweet babes.

His deep blues opened wide in the morning dew,
looking up to the mirror of his soul, he smiled;
fingers deep into the bottomless pockets,
remembering the marbles lost day before,
treasures filled his little chest with giggles.

He would be king someday and live up above,
like his father before him, in a royal shack,
made for a fisherman without a pole,
a warrior without armor, leaking pearls
from clouds that cried tears of joy for him.

No prison to be built for the sprouting imagination,
or boundaries for a love greater than his whole kin's
in awe they will soon raise a wondering gaze,
when he takes flight to another world he made,
and ask whence his immense power came.

A little sorry, as alone in numbers they must remain,
the dream killers cannot survive the enchantment,
searching stone and brick, to build fortresses,
isolated, safe from the threat of possible awe,
their prince free, cries for them, for it is too late.

Dreams of Men

Crossing the old DMZ not far from the country club
I encounter the same despair on a rusty bicycle.

A humanoid covered in colored skins not his
crosses the avenue unaware of the speeding Humvee.

Behind, he leaves the scantily dressed girl of the night puffing
on the cheap menthols, in waiting of her next date.

She misses nothing, her eye on the loiterer sipping
on what's left of a jumbo container of rancid wine.

The rose on her chest is making way to a new wrinkle
and she coughs up a thick past of tar and sorrow.

In this tepid loneliness, passers-by still smile a little
for they seek one more slice of hope in the corner store.

They did save a few pennies on those rare luxuries
to invest in a sure bet for a few lottery tickets.

There they live, cast away by the world outside
there they die without regret for this forsaken life.

Witness to their many failures a nameless friend
collapsed on the concrete vanishes beneath his filth.

Monument to an age in ruins he is but a corpse
inhaling a mixture of what humanity spews.

Tomorrow he will be stored away without a tear
to be remembered only by the stench of his disease.

The gambler, the drunk, the whore next door soon to follow
devoured by simple dreams never to be achieved.

Prisoners of imposed vices their only belongings,
never were they to shake those shackles of destiny.

Dying with the Evening Gown

Standing before the long mirror she wondered
to hide this nakedness in the dark of fancy velour
or to wrap those limbs in worn-out denim.

Cocktails to be served at five in the eve
in a room ornate with illustrious chandeliers
imported crystals shining of artificial suns.

Boasting pearls, diamonds, and rubies she descended
princess among royalty in make-believe worlds
her breast heaved with the power of intimate convictions.

A deep breath held within her chest
pleading for patience in a room stuffed with smoke
pretenses and empty vanity she dreamed of freedom.

Perhaps another would appear rejected next door
too attached to the liberty of youthful years
choosing instead to shred the tuxedos of success.

She imagines herself atop desolate islands
near and far without lace, precious metals, or fame
free in a white shroud dedicated to the world.

Mingling with the semblances of peers
they brush against the pure skin of her innocence
unable to make contact as she continues to the gates.

A gaze constant upon the abandoned domains
her soul smiles for she steps into her dream
made of pains joys and true healings.

Without a look back to those well-dressed ghosts
she shed the million-dollar evening gown
to enter as upon her birth within a fitting kingdom.

Easy to Die

Lives move at the pace of a blur
he sits in the café with a large drink
stunned by the ghosts all around.

None will stop for a mere flash
too busy as they are in futile motions
in herds small or large yet alone

The funeral cortege swings by, surrounded
with the gyrating colors of the flag
under relentless rains cold as ice.

So many have traversed the city
following the route to oblivion leaving
skid marks in the blacktop for a legacy.

If only they had had time to prepare
to compose a symphony even to the wind
for an echo to remember them into eternity.

But they chose to suffer without meaning
speeding through the days bequeathed them
unaware of the darkness when they come to the end.

If only they knew how easy it is to die
when you have written a story upon the night
another chapter added to the tale of the universe.

Electronic Chef

Rest at last
I have been spinning for hours
at the touch of a fingertip

I believe it is a fever coming
perhaps a touch of the flu
please let me sleep a moment

The dings have become tiresome
they echo so loudly in my chambers
with the light so bright.

So much for my pause
no union fights my war
here come my regulars.

Sisters in crime, souls in learning
their eyes stare, wonder, ponder
will it be two, three, four, or more?

I have had enough of teas, coffees, and corn
I want something else on my menu
what have they brought today?

Spaghetti? Lasagna? Oh No! ramen it is
how can they, how dare they?
don't they know I was born in Michigan?!

They laugh, they giggle and chit-chat with the master
sitting at his throne like the tyrant of ages
a thumb comes, so close, too close, and…

There I go spinning again, humming my old tune
under the strobes, my headache is back
if only I could reach the waves of the sea.

Empty beds

They sat quietly in geography
watching the slow flow of the Nile
dreaming of future journeys into adulthood
fifteen minutes from recess and a game of catch
instead, they slipped into history unexpected.

Bags packed for summertime
will remain locked as memento to childish hopes
days from the beaches of the gulf
their bodies pale under neon lights
tan lines fading into ghostly night.

They boarded the big yellow with laughter
oblivious to the evil that lurked near them
an eighteen-year-old heart of ice
armed with the hate he manufactured
thinking that was better than invisibility.

The summer dresses won't be coming home tonight
the cleats will stay in rusty lockers
flags will fly somewhere near the ground
no one will be able to dry the torrents of grief
once more shed in the name of freedom.

Ending

Walking in a fierce storm of daggers and blades,
fighting tornadoes, hurricanes, and earthquakes,
no overcoat, nor hat, not even the sturdy umbrella
will resist the changes which come with the storms.

Layer after layer, the fortress must collapse,
and leave way for the elements to erode at last;
what may have remained of a dying ray of hope,
arms clutched on a weakening chest in a final attempt.

Each step more arduous while the grimaces arise,
more violent with pain flashing like lightning,
through a crumbling pack of bones, flesh collapsing,
he is nearing the end, as soon, the knees will fail.

Fingers levitate perhaps, or is it mere illusion,
as the eyes filling with dust, sand, and tears
no longer certain of the vision so tender, beloved,
appears unattainable, but which is less real?

It is done, as he stops, bewildered by a last snap frigid,
a last glance from her soul as her path seems pleasant
rays of warm light shine upon this royal presence,
hail continues to shatter the scenery for the observer.

A curtain raises to the skies, made of steel and stone,
transparent as if to enhance the suffering of him,
as he stays behind frozen, effigy to all lost dreams,
but he will not vanish, his agony must be prolonged.

She too continues to be, her step confident and adored,
nonchalant always; her figure keeps the same stature;
tortured by the impossibility, he is condemned to be
the spectator, as she gleefully goes on her solitary days.

Patience

Like a statue held mysterious upon the blue
in deep sleep grabbing the memories
wearing the shadows of the changing hour
wrinkled, patched, stained, it is.

The nail chipped with each new day
holds on tight to a meaning deep
yet life requires little space.

Nearby the walking stick teases, tempts, longs
one day found upon a country hike
thus forever friends it asks why
upon the blue, it too must await.

Of the old tree, oak of a hundred years
it wears the deep scars of many worries
its veins tracing the paths taken
and the knots still tighten with its loves lost.

A worn sleeve seems to reach down to offer comfort
to crowd its solitude absolute
while a salute from above tipping slightly
one old peasant to another hello.

Like a time beaten Lab begging for the mud
the ice and snow of the harshest February
the measly panoply of three sings in unison
to a chance meeting in Heaven's meadow.

Upon the solid blue, unchanged, asleep, peaceful
the old coat, the hat, and the walking stick
in deep converse, reminisce of the rain, the sleet
the storms, the lighting, and the sun to be no more.

Hopeful they conspire in the dark night chamber
fearful of the armoire of old, the stairs to a world too remote
so far away to leave in their folds and warts, a glimmer of hope
still, they remain, not to awaken suspicion in the new tenant.

What plans for a future may they make?
Is their destiny done, their journey at port?
They hang on to hope, on the nails to the blue,
at attention, for one last tour in the garden.

To once more commune with the fragrant ones
revel in the burst of Spring colors, in spite of the pain
of the Earth's work, kneeling, bending, sighing
ignoring the burning, the hail, and the chapped dreams.

They stand at ready, spying for the familiar hinges to cringe
the beloved slipper sliding to announce again life
animated group of kindergartners at playtime
to celebrate his return, their teacher, their pal.

Parking lot

Bass bearing earthquakes to another land
shaking rust of a collapsing carriage
the glass broken to a private chaos
his head a mirror to azure skies
oxymoronic slogans upon dilapidated stickers
he drives a little planet of nonsensical mismatches.

The realm is grand of melting asphalt
vibrating with the march of so many monsters
skeletons of ancient steel and contemporary vinyl
lost in the midst of this horrid stampede
a lost traveler ponders the colorful sight
overwhelmed by incomprehensible dialects.

A swirl throws scribbles into the spheres
some he may collect as token of faraway journeys
turning to absorb the sordid spectacle
he might fall beneath the terrifying wheels
knight without armor he almost encounters his own demise
surrounded by a formless humanoid mob.

The familiar site of the one in search of sustenance
an eve spent in the anthill of his peers
he wonders at the rainbow of these entities
sparring for a life too precious to be noted
why would a man speak so many tongues
yet remain a stranger to his many very words.

It is a surprising realm born so far from this earth
populated by similar species so distant
oozing as if molasses from Hades's depths
perhaps it will devour him also as he gazes
into an abyss racing to the horizon
irrelevant to the innumerable hearts about.